The best and most
beautiful things in the
world cannot be seen
nor even touched, but
just felt with the heart.

— ANNE SULLIVAN

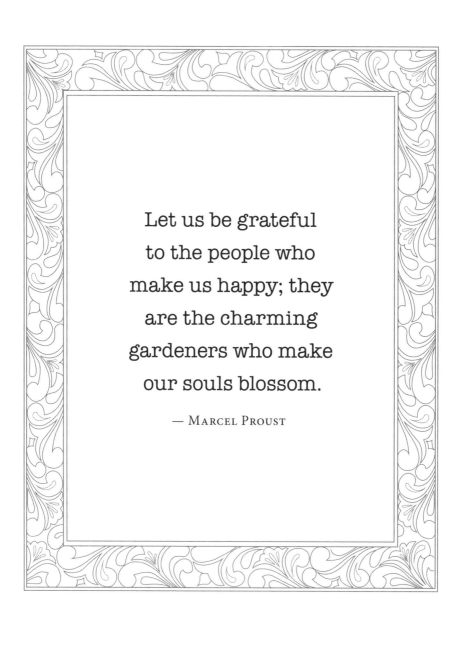

Let us be grateful
to the people who
make us happy; they
are the charming
gardeners who make
our souls blossom.

— Marcel Proust

Happiness. — A butterfly, which when pursued, seems always just beyond your grasp; but if you sit down quietly, may alight upon you.

— *The Daily Crescent*, "A Chapter of Definitions", June 1848

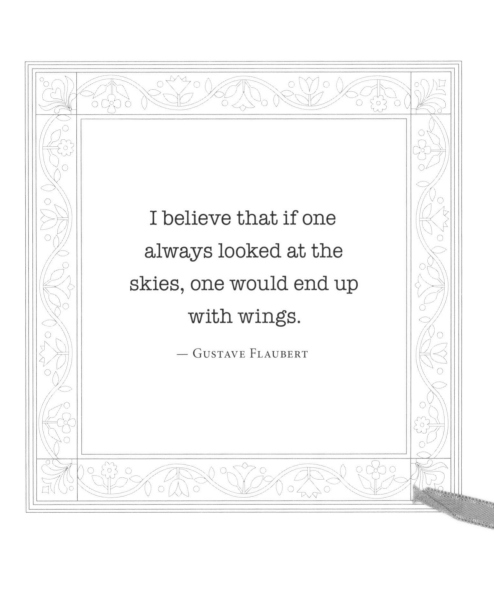

I believe that if one
always looked at the
skies, one would end up
with wings.

— GUSTAVE FLAUBERT

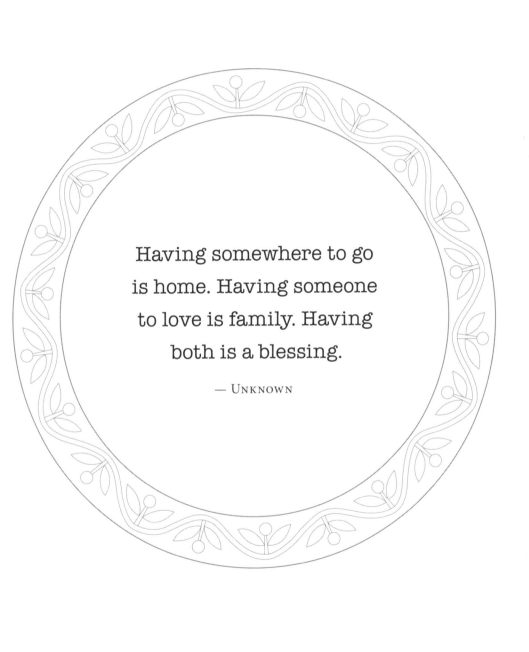

Having somewhere to go
is home. Having someone
to love is family. Having
both is a blessing.

— Unknown

Intense love does not
measure, it just gives.

— MOTHER TERESA

Alone, we can
do so little;
together, we can do
so much.

— HELEN KELLER

All you need is love.
But a little chocolate now
and then doesn't hurt.

— CHARLES SCHULZ

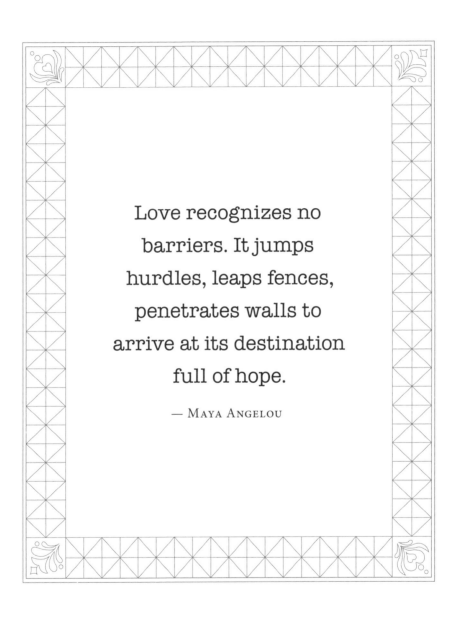

Love recognizes no
barriers. It jumps
hurdles, leaps fences,
penetrates walls to
arrive at its destination
full of hope.

— MAYA ANGELOU

It didn't matter how big
our house was;
it mattered that there
was love in it.

— PETER BUFFETT,
LIFE IS WHAT YOU MAKE IT

A single rose can be
my garden; a single
friend, my world.

— Leo Buscaglia

Spread love everywhere
you go. Let no one ever
come to you without
leaving happier.

— MOTHER TERESA

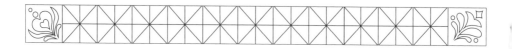

About Jim Shore

Jim Shore grew up in rural South Carolina, the son of artistic parents who instilled a love of American folk art. His grandmother was a master quilter who taught him the patience and skill to bring intricate designs to life. Jim worked for decades developing his craft, manufacturing his own designs, and traveling the country to sell his work. Finally, in 2001, he partnered with Enesco to create Heartwood Creek, the successful brand that brought Jim worldwide fame. Jim has received multiple awards from prestigious trade organizations, including the ICON HONORS Life Accomplishment Award in 2012. Through his partnership with Enesco, the Jim Shore Collection has grown from a small group of Santas, snowmen, and angels to a broad year-round brand respected and sold around the world. Jim's boundless creativity and unique ability enable him to touch people in all walks of life through his art.

ISBN 978-1-64178-116-9

Fox Chapel Publishing makes every effort to use environmentally friendly paper for printing.

We are always looking for talented authors and artists. To submit an idea, please send a brief inquiry to acquisitions@foxchapelpublishing.com.

Printed in Singapore
First printing